NEW FRIENDS, NEW LANGUAGES

Karen Nemeth and Diego Jiménez Manzano

Supporting home languages and learning new languages together!

KN

I dedicate this book to dedicated early childhood teachers who love children and all their languages.

DJM

Special thanks to my family. I wish to dedicate this book to my mother, María.

Language Castle Press
PO Box 883
Newtown, PA 18940
languagecastlepress@gmail.com

Copyright 2022 by Karen Nemeth

All rights reserved. No part of this book may be reproduced in any form without permission in writing from the author, except in the case of brief quotations embodied in critical articles or reviews.

ISBN: 978-0-9899899-4-7

New Friends, New Languages

Karen Nemeth and Diego Jiménez Manzano

Good morning, children!
Welcome to our school!
says Teacher Nan.

Teacher Nan

Saleem

Wyatt

Violet

Theo

Here is our classroom, says Teacher Nan. We are all friends who speak different languages.

Saleem speaks Arabic. Violet speaks Chinese. Wyatt speaks Spanish. Heather, Theo, Vivi and I speak English. We will learn the languages of our friends so we can learn and play together.

Heather

Vivi

I see lots of interesting play, says Teacher Nan.

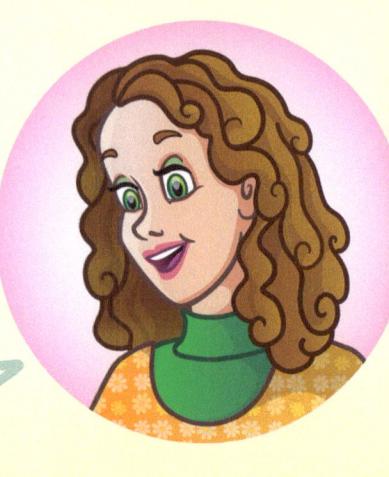

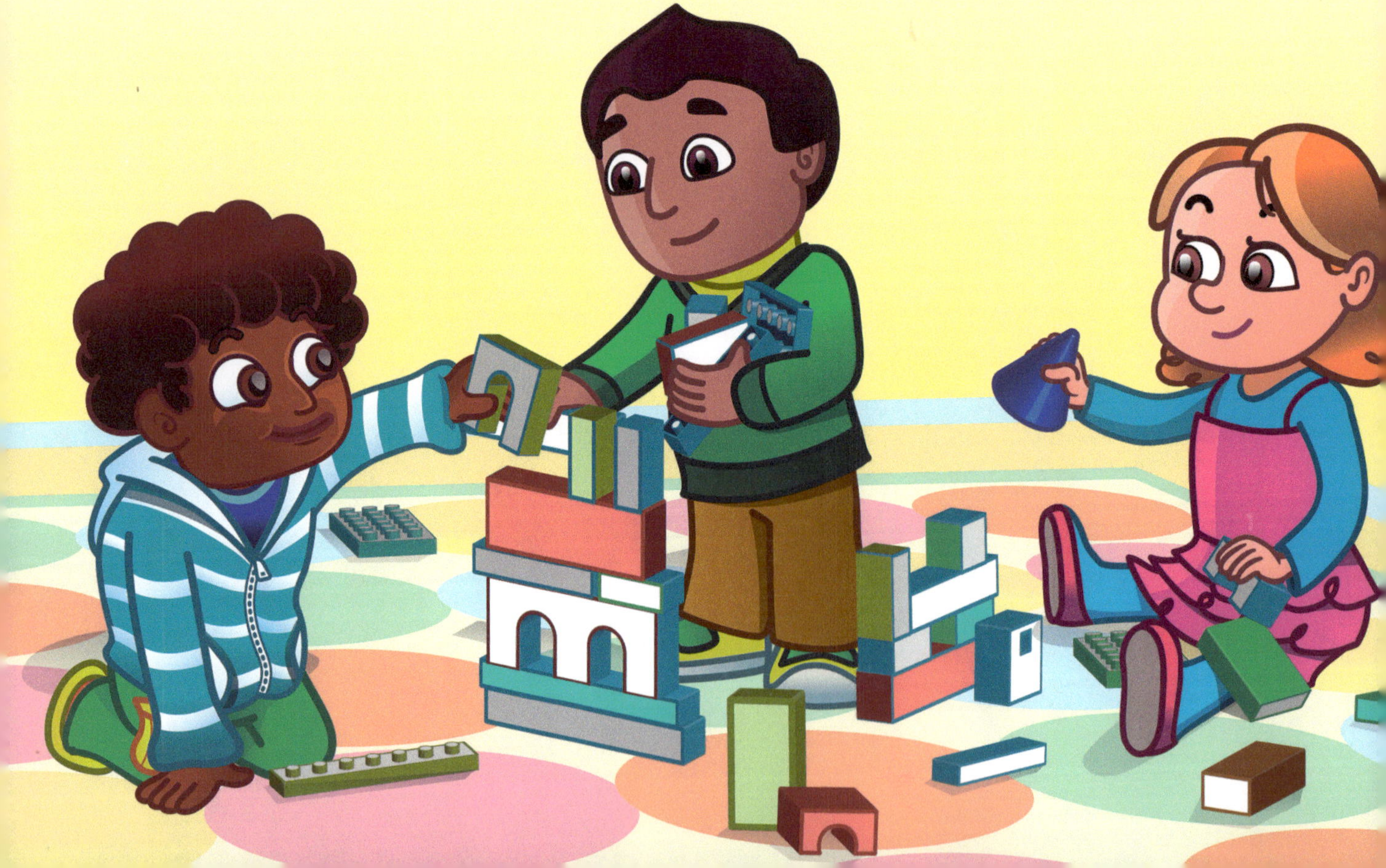

New Friends, New Languages Word List

These words and phrases will support a welcoming environment for children who speak English, Spanish, Chinese and Arabic.

The child-appropriate translations and phonetic spellings are designed to help adults and children communicate and learn together in different languages. There are lots of ways to use this list.

Visit www.languagecastle.com to share your own creative ideas!

- Invite family members to record themselves pronouncing the words so you can learn to say them too.
- Make enlarged copies of these pages to post as reminders around the room.
- Build your relationship with each child by trying to use some of these key words in his or her home language.
- Show the children where a phrase appears in the book and then see if they can say it in more than one language.
- Project some words onto a whiteboard and invite children to teach you and their friends to identify and pronounce the words they know.
- Encourage children to study the features of how each language looks and sounds by using phrases that have the same meaning.
- Invite children to make a skit or puppet show using some of the words in a new language.
- Bring families, friends and volunteers together to add to this list of words and practice using the new words together.

English	Spanish	Chinese	Arabic	Add a language
I'm scared.	Tengo miedo.	我很害怕。 Wǒ hěn hài pà.	أنا خائف. 'Ana kha'if	
Welcome	Bienvenidos	欢迎 Huān yíng	أهلاً بكم ahlan bikum	
We are all friends who speak different languages.	Todos somos amigos que hablamos idiomas diferentes	我们都是说不同语言的朋友。 Wǒ men dōu shì shuō bu tóng yǔyán de péng yǒu.	نحن جميعًا أصدقاء نتحدث لغات مختلفة. naHnu jami'an 'asdiqaun nataHaddathu lughaatan mukhtalifatan	
Can I play with you?	¿Puedo jugar contigo?	我可以跟你玩吗？ Wǒ kě yǐ gēn nǐ wán ma?	هل يمكنني اللعب معك؟ hel yumkinuni 'al'abu ma'aka?	
Yes, let's play.	Sí, vamos a jugar.	好的,我们玩吧。 Hǎo de, wǒmen wán ba.	نعم، هيا نلعب سويًا. na'am haya nal'ab sawiyya.	
Tidy up.	Recoger.	整理吧。 Zhěng lǐ ba.	استعدوا. astaeduu.	
Do you need help?	¿Necesitas ayuda?	你需要帮忙吗？ Nǐ xū yào bāng máng ma?	هل تحتاج إلى مساعدة؟ hal taHtaj ila musa'ada?	
Bathroom	El baño	洗手间 Xǐshǒujiān ma	الحمام al-Hammam	

English	Spanish	Chinese	Arabic	Add a language
A drink	Una bebida	喝水吗 Hē shuǐ ma	المشروب Al mashrub	
Food	Comida	吃东西吗 Chī dōng xi ma	الطعام Al ta'am	
Rest	Descansar	休息吗 Xiū xí ma	الستراحة Al istiraHa	
Thank you.	Gracias.	谢谢。 Xiè xiè.	شكرًا لكم. shukran lakum.	
What is This?	¿Qué es esto?	这是什么? Zhè shì shén me?	ما هذا؟! ma hatha?	
What will happen next?	¿Qué pasará después?	接下来会发生什么? Jiē xià lái huì fā shēng shén me?	ماذا سيحدث بعد ذلك؟ matha sayaHduth ba'd zalek?	
Tell me about this.	Háblame de esto	告诉我。 Gào su wǒ.	أخبرني عن هذا الموضوع. 'akhbarani 'an hathal mowdhoo'	
Play time	Recreo	游戏时间。 Yóu xì shí jiān.	وقت اللعب waqt alla'ib.	
Stop. Be careful	Para. Ten cuidado.	停。小心。 Tíng. Xiǎo xīn.	توقفوا والتزموا الحذر. tawaqafuu wailtazimuu alHathar.	

English	Spanish	Chinese	Arabic	Add a language
I will see you tomorrow.	Te veo mañana.	明天见。 Míng tiān jiàn.	أراكم غداً. 'arakum ghadan.	
Goodbye	Adiós	再见。 Zài jiàn.	مع السلامة. ma'al salama	
Chinese	chino	中文 Zhōng wén	اللغة الصينية. 'alogha alSiniya	
English	inglés	英语 Yīngyǔ	اللغة الإنجليزية. 'alogha al'iinjlizia	
Arabic	árabe	阿拉伯语 Ā lā bó yǔ	اللغة العربية. 'alogha alarabia	
Spanish	español	西班牙语 Xī bān yá yǔ	اللغة الإسبانية. 'alogha alisbaniya	
I am your teacher.	Soy tu maestra	我是你的老师。 Wǒ shì nǐ de lǎo shī.	أنا معلمتكم. ana mu'allimata kum.	
I will take good care of you.	Te cuidaré muy bien.	我会照顾好你。 Wǒ huì zhào gù hǎo nǐ.	سوف أرعاكم رعاية جيدة. sofa 'ar'aakum ri'aya jayiida	

www.ingramcontent.com/pod-product-compliance
Lightning Source LLC
Chambersburg PA
CBHW041437010526
44118CB00002B/107